BLOOD
AND GUTS
and
RATS' TAIL
PIZZA

BLOOD
AND GUTS
and
RATS' TAIL PIZZA

Vivian French

Illustrated by
Chris Fisher

Orion
Children's Books

First published in Great Britain in 2013 by Orion Children's Books
a division of the Orion Publishing Group Ltd
Orion House
5 Upper Saint Martin's Lane
London WC2H 9EA
An Hachette UK Company

1 3 5 7 9 10 8 6 4 2

The Orion Publishing Group's policy is to use papers that are
natural, renewable and recyclable products and made from wood
grown in sustainable forests. The logging and manufacturing
processes are expected to conform to the environmental regulations
of the country of origin.

A catalogue record for this book is available from the British Library.

ISBN 978 1 4440 0729 9

Printed in China

www.orionbooks.co.uk

For Nat (of course)
and for Chris and Chris as well -
with much love

Contents

Chapter One   11

Chapter Two   23

Chapter Three   39

Chapter Four   51

Chapter Five   67

Chapter One

The Blood and Guts Café was
open.

Big Billy Bones, the owner, was snoring behind the counter.

Cruncher the dog was asleep under a table.

Hank was staring out of the window.

There were no customers.
Hank opened the door and looked out. The street was empty.

"That's weird," said Hank.

He looked up at the sign in the window.

Slug and Snail stew.
(Lovely crunchy shells)

Rats' tail pizza
(ten tails on each slice)

Scrambled worms on toast. (all burned black)

Saturday special!!!
Guts pie with Blood Sauce

P.S. Absolutely
NO GIRLS!

Hank wiped the sign with a cloth. Big Billy Bones didn't like girls.

Hank agreed. He had five sisters, and he had to wait to use the bathroom every single morning.

He gave 'Absolutely No Girls' an extra polish, then looked out of the door again. The street was still empty.

"VERY weird," said Hank.

He shut the door and went into the kitchen.

The stew was bubbling on the cooker. The pies were in the oven. The rats' tail pizzas were laid out in rows. The worms were wriggling in a bowl.

Hank went to see Big Billy.

"Please, Sir," he said. "What should I do? There's nobody here."

Big Billy Bones woke up and frowned. Big Billy only looked happy when his café was full of customers.

"Nobody here? Why not?"

"I don't know," said Hank.

"Then go and find out," said Big Billy. "No customers means no money. No money means no job. If you want your job, get going."

Hank and Cruncher walked down the road.

"There's Spotty Pete's house," said Hank. "He comes every day for Slug and Snail stew."

"Woof!" said Cruncher.

Hank rang the doorbell
There was no answer.

Hank and Cruncher walked to
Three Legs Larry's cottage.

"Larry always wants
scrambled worms," said Hank.

"Woof!" said Cruncher.

Hank knocked on the door.
There was no answer.

Hank and Cruncher went
round the corner ... and stopped.

"Look!" Hank said. "There's Spotty Pete and Three Legs Larry and Fingers Fred!"

Cruncher wagged his tail. "Woof!"

"They're eating!" said Hank. "They're eating ... cake!"

Chapter Two

Hank rubbed his eyes.

Pete and Larry and Fred were sitting outside a café, but there had never been a café there before.

The café was on wheels, and the tables were outside. Tables with fancy table cloths, and chairs with fancy cushions.

"Hi, Hank!" Pete shouted. "Come and have some cake!"

Hank came closer. There
was a sign above the window.

Mighty Millie's
Travelling Cake
Shop

"Hi, Hank!" Larry waved at
him. "Come and try a Dainty
Daisy Cupcake! They're
yummy!"

Fred rubbed his tummy. "Ug."

"Millie?" Hank thought.
"Huh! Just like a girl to steal
our customers."

A big hairy monster came
out of the café.

"That's Mighty Millie," Pete
whispered.

Beside Mighty Millie was a much smaller hairy monster.

"Hello, boy, I'm Little Mo," she said. "Want some cake?"

"No," said Hank. "I don't like girls and I don't like cake."

"Fancy that," said Mighty Millie. "All girls and all cake?"

Hank scowled. "I don't like girls who steal Big Billy Bones' customers."

"And I don't like rude boys," said Little Mo. She tipped the jug over Hank's head. "Try some Buttercup Custard."

"Ooooof!" spluttered Hank.
"Ooooof!"

Pete, Larry and Fred
laughed. Cruncher barked
loudly.

Hank sneezed. "Atchoo! I'm going to tell Big Billy Bones!"

"We'll be shaking in our shoes," Little Mo said. "Nipper! Come here!"

A very little dog came running round the corner.

"Nipper," said Little Mo. "Chase them!"

"Yip!" said Nipper, and he nipped Hank's ankles.

"Ow!" yelled Hank. "Ow! Nipper bit Cruncher's tail.

"Yowl" howled Cruncher.

Hank ran, and Cruncher ran too.

Nipper ran after them. "Yip! Yip! Yip!"

They ran all the way back to the Blood and Guts café.

Big Billy Bones stared at him.
"What's that dripping off the end of your nose?" he asked.

"Buttercup Custard," said Hank.

"Buttercup Custard? Yuck!"
said Big Billy. "Did you find
our customers?"

Hank nodded. "They were
eating cake. With girls."

"What?" roared Big Billy.

Hank nodded again as he wiped his nose and licked his fingers.

"They've gone to a **cake** shop? With **girls?**" Big Billy growled.

Hank wasn't listening.

He was licking his fingers. "Hey, Big Billy! This tastes amazing!"

"Won't be any good," said Big Billy. Not if it's made by girls."

"Just try it," Hank said.

Big Billy scooped a blob from behind Hank's ear and put his finger in his mouth. A slow smile spread across his face.

"By my ding dong trousers, you're right. That custard's the best! Off you go, boy!"

Hank stared. "Go where?"

"To find out how to make Buttercup Custard. Think of it...

Slug and Snail Stew with Buttercup Custard.

Rats' Tail Pizza with Buttercup Custard.

Scrambled worms with Buttercup Custard.

Guts Pie with Blood Sauce and Buttercup Custard!

Why, we'd make our
fortune! I want that custard,
and I want it now."

Chapter Three

Hank sighed. He looked out of the window. Nipper was chasing Cruncher round and round the café.

Then Hank had an idea.

He went to fetch a rats' tail pizza from the kitchen.

"Here, boy!" Hank opened the door. "Look! Lovely pizza!"

"Yip?" yapped Nipper.

"Woof?" barked Cruncher.

"Come and get it!" said Hank.
As the dogs dashed into the
café, Hank slammed the door
shut.

"Got you!"

Hank sat down and wrote
a letter.

Dear Little Mo,
I have got your dog,
Nipper.
You can have him
back **IF** you tell me
how to make buttercup
custard. Hank.

"Cruncher! Here, boy!"

Cruncher came to see what Hank wanted. Nipper gobbled up the last crumbs of pizza.

Hank tied the letter to Cruncher's collar.

"Woof?" asked Cruncher.

Hank frowned. How could he open the door without letting Nipper out?

He went into the kitchen to fetch another pizza.

"Yip!" Nipper followed him.

"Good dog!" Hank put the pizza on the floor.

Nipper was too busy eating to notice as Hank shut him in the kitchen.

Hank patted Cruncher's
head. "Take the letter to Little
Mo! Off you go!"

Cruncher nodded. "Woof!"

Hank sat down outside
the café, and waited.

He waited ...

and he waited.

And then he saw Little Mo
walking towards the Blood
and Guts Café.

Hurrah! thought Hank.
She's come to tell me how to
make Buttercup Custard!

But she hadn't.

"You think you're SO clever," Little Mo said. "You've got Nipper, but you forgot something. We've got Cruncher! And we won't let him go until you bring back Nipper and say you're sorry."

Little Mo looked at the sign.

"Absolutely no girls?
Huh! Just like a boy to write
something silly like that. Well,
let me tell you something. I
hate boys."

She turned round and
marched back up the road.

Chapter Four

Hank paced up and down.

If I can't make Buttercup Custard, we won't have any customers. If we don't have any customers, I won't have a job.

But I love Cruncher. He's the best dog ever, and he's my friend – I have to get him back, even if I do have to say I'm sorry to that girl.

Hank stopped. He'd thought of something else.

It's all my fault that Little Mo's got Cruncher. Maybe I wasn't so clever after all.

In the kitchen, Nipper was lying on his back. He looked very fat.

The stew pan was empty. There were no rats' tail pizzas. The bowl of worms was upside down. The oven door was open, and every pie was gone.

"Wow," said Hank. "Wow!"

"Burp," said Nipper.

"Come on, Nipper. You're going home," said Hank.

Nipper shook his head.
"Don't you want to go home?" Hank asked.
Nipper shook his head again.

Hank put Nipper under his arm and walked out of the café and down the road.

He walked all the way to Mighty Millie's Travelling Cake Shop.

Little Mo was tidying up.
She put down her cloth.

"Have you come to say
you're sorry?" she asked.

"Yes." said Hank. "Here's
Nipper, and I don't want to
know about Buttercup Custard.
I just want Cruncher back."

"Really?" Mo looked surprised.

"Really," said Hank.

He put Nipper down. Nipper didn't move.

"Nipper!" Little Mo looked even more surprised. "Don't you want to say hello?"

Nipper shook his head.

"Mum!" Little Mo shouted. "Mum! Nipper's here and he's not right!"

Mighty Millie came outside. "What have you done to my dog?" she said.

"Nothing," said Hank. "He did eat a lot of pies though. And worms. And rats' tail pizzas. And all my Slug and Snail Stew."

"Did you **really** eat all those things, Nipper?" Mighty Millie asked.

Nipper nodded.

"Well I never." Millie looked at Hank. "Nipper's fussy. You must be a good cook."

"We used to sell out every Saturday," Hank told her.

"Hank's Slug and Snail Stew is yummy," said Pete.

"The Scrambled Worms are scrummy," said Larry.

"Didn't you sell out today?"
asked Little Mo.

"No," said Hank. "Nobody
came. They all came here
instead."

"I see." Mighty Millie nodded.
"Wait here!"

She opened the door of her Cake Shop.

Cruncher came bursting out. "Woof!" he barked. "Woof!"

"Hello, boy," said Hank, and he hugged Cruncher. "Let's go home."

"Just a minute." Little Mo pulled a piece of paper out of her apron pocket. "Haven't you forgotten something?"

"Forgotten what?" said Hank.

Mo handed him the paper. "Here. Now you can make Buttercup Custard."

"Thank you!" said Hank.

Little Mo looked at Hank. "We don't like boys who are rude. We do like boys who like dogs."

"And we do like boys who can cook," said Mighty Millie.

Hank went very red. "I'm sorry I was rude," he said. "Maybe ... maybe SOME girls are OK."

"And maybe SOME boys are OK," said Little Mo.

Buttercup Custard
· 20 buttercups
· milk
· 6 Eggs
· sugar
· cornflour

Chapter Five

Hank walked along the road with Cruncher beside him.

"We'll have to tell Big Billy Bones, Cruncher," he said. "Girls aren't all bad. They make the best custard, that's for sure!"

"Woof!" said Cruncher.

"Yip!" Nipper ran after them.

"Go home, Nipper," said Hank.

Hank picked up Nipper and took him back.

"Thanks," said Little Mo.

Hank and Cruncher set off down the road again.

"Yip!" Nipper ran after them.

"Go home, Nipper," said Hank.

Hank picked up Nipper and took him back again.

"Thanks," said Mighty Millie.

Nipper began to howl.

"Yowl! Yowl! Yowl!!!!!"

Millie scratched her hairy
head. Mo pulled at her pigtails.
Hank rubbed his nose.

None of them knew what
to do.

"Hmmm ... " Hank had an idea, but he wasn't sure if it was a good one.

Big Billy didn't like girls. But Big Billy did want Buttercup Custard. And he did want his customers back...

"Maybe," he said slowly,
"maybe we could cook
together? Your cake shop is on
wheels. You could park next to
our café."

"Yip!" Nipper jumped up and
down.

"Woof!" barked Cruncher.

"OK," said Mighty Millie. "It's
a deal." She and Hank shook
hands.

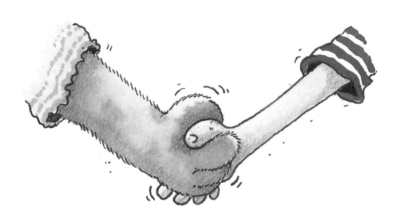

So Pete, Larry and Fred
rolled Mighty Millie's Travelling
Cake Shop along the road.

They stopped right next to
the Blood and Guts Café.

The door of the Blood and Guts Café opened, and Big Billy Bones stepped out. "Do I see girls?" he growled.

Hank swallowed nervously. "They're going to make us Buttercup Custard. Loads and loads of Buttercup Custard," he said.

There was a long pause, then Big Billy Bones nodded.

"That's all right then," he said.

Slug and Snail stew -
Rats' tail pizza -
Scrambled worms on toast
SATURDAY SPECIAL!!!
Guts Pie with Blood Sauce
ALL with Mighty Millie's
extra-special super delicious
Buttercup CUSTARD!!
ps Try one of Mighty Millie's
teeny weeny Posie Posy Pies for
Pudding. They're the BEST!
PPS ALL girls
welcome!

The café and cake shop
were full to bursting

and so were the customers.

What are you going to read next?

More adventures with

or go to sea with

Horrid Henry,

Poppy the Pirate Dog,

or into space with

You could have fun on

Cudweed.

A Rainbow Shopping Day,

or explore

Down in the Jungle,